Talking Turkey

and Other Clichés We Say

by Nancy Loewen

illustrated by Adam Watkins

PICTURE WINDOW BOOKS
a capstone imprint

What is a cliché?

To my wife, Amy, and daughter, Lucy—A.W.

Editor: Jill Kalz
Designer: Lori Bye
Art Director: Nathan Gassman
Production Specialist: Michelle Biedscheid
The illustrations in this book were created with water color, pen, and ink.

Picture Window Books
151 Good Counsel Drive
P.O. Box 669
Mankato, MN 56002-0669
877-845-8392
www.capstonepub.com

Library of Congress Cataloging-in-Publication Data
Loewen, Nancy, 1964-
  Talking turkey and other clichés we say / by Nancy Loewen ; illustrated by
Adam Watkins.
    p. cm. — (Ways to say it)
  Includes index.
  ISBN 978-1-4048-6272-2 (library binding) — ISBN 978-1-4048-6716-1 (paperback)
  1. English language–Idioms–Juvenile literature. 2. Clichés–Juvenile literature.
I. Watkins, Adam, ill. II. Title.
  PE1460.L596 2011
  428.1–dc22
                                                    2010033769

Special thanks to our adviser, Terry Flaherty, PhD,
Professor of English, Minnesota State University, Mankato,
for his expertise.

Printed in the United States of America in North Mankato, Minnesota.
072011   006231CGVMI

You might say that a cliché is
old news.

A cliché is a phrase that people use a lot.
When the phrase was new, it was unusual and
interesting. The people who first said it were
thinking outside the box. But now
we don't even notice common clichés.

Sometimes it's fine to use clichés. Other times, we might
want to find a new way to say what we're thinking.

It goes without saying, clichés are here to stay!

Meet Trish.

Meet Faye.

Trish and Faye do everything together. They are

true blue

friends.

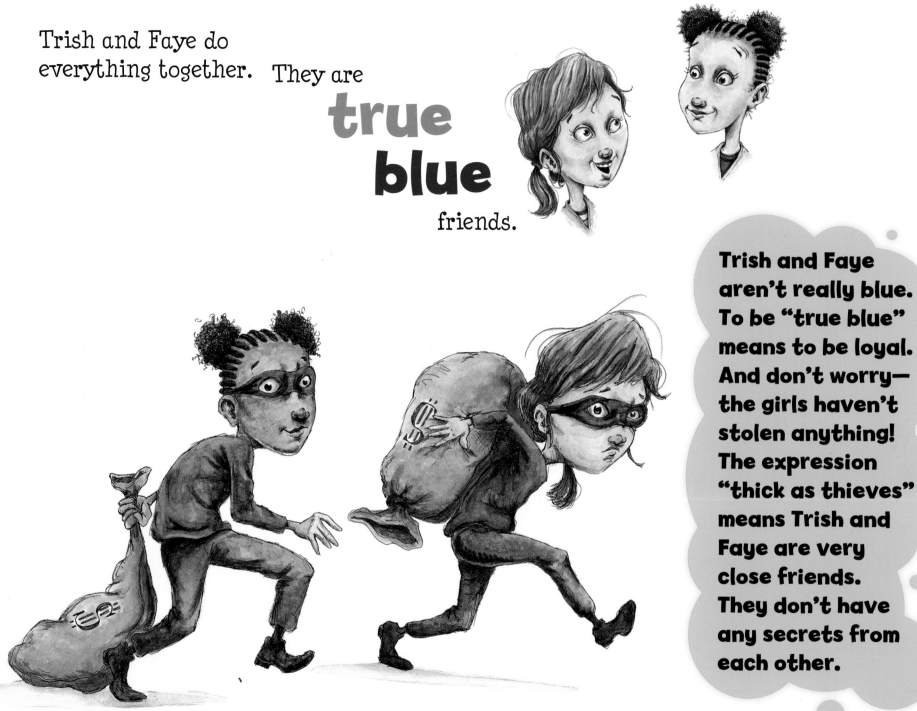

Trish and Faye aren't really blue. To be "true blue" means to be loyal. And don't worry—the girls haven't stolen anything! The expression "thick as thieves" means Trish and Faye are very close friends. They don't have any secrets from each other.

Everyone says the girls are **thick as thieves.**

Today is a big day for Trish and Faye. The Bonus Brothers are giving a concert at the fair!

Their new song

knocks Trish's socks off!

Many clichés are idioms. Idioms don't make sense when we look at the actual meaning of the words. But because we're so familiar with the phrases, we understand what's being said. Here we know that this is an important day for Trish and Faye. We also know that they really like the Bonus Brothers!

If one's "socks are knocked off," it means he or she is amazed. The expression has been used since the mid-1800s.

The Whiplash

In the morning, Trish and Faye ride the Whiplash. They **SCREAM** AT THE TOP OF THEIR **LUNGS.**

"Do you still have the tickets?" Trish asks Faye.

Clichés often exaggerate to create an effect. Which ride would you rather go on: the one that makes you "scream" or the one that makes you "scream at the very top of your lungs"?

"You bet I do," Faye says.

For lunch, Trish buys a sloppy joe.
And for dessert? Cotton candy!

Trish has a SWEET TOOTH.

CANDY

The idiom "sweet tooth" has been in use since
the late 1300s. Originally it referred to liking
any kind of special, fancy food, not just sweets.

Trish's tooth isn't sweet—she just likes to eat sweet things. Faye's eyes are perfectly normal. She just bought more food than she could eat.

Faye buys three hot dogs and a milk shake. She can't finish it all.

Her EYES ARE **BIGGER** THAN HER **STOMACH.**

"Do you still have the tickets?" Trish asks.

"You can't be too careful."

Some clichés are proverbs. A proverb is a short, helpful saying. When Trish says, "You can't be too careful," she's really saying, "Don't lose those tickets!" But the proverb sounds a little nicer.

Faye gives her

A
THUMBS
UP.

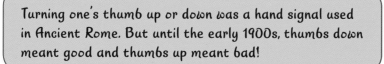

Turning one's thumb up or down was a hand signal used in Ancient Rome. But until the early 1900s, thumbs down meant good and thumbs up meant bad!

Next Trish and Faye go to the petting zoo.

They **let the cat out of the bag.**

People have been "letting (or not letting) cats out of bags" since the mid-1700s. The phrase refers to dishonest salespeople who tricked buyers by putting cats in bags, instead of more valuable animals.

DO NOT DISTURB

They let sleeping dogs lie.

"Let sleeping dogs lie" is a proverb from the 1200s. It warned against waking up fierce watchdogs.

14

They **GO ON A WILD GOOSE CHASE.**

"Going on a wild goose chase" is a horse-racing phrase from the 1500s. Riders followed a leader in a pattern that looked like geese in flight.

While Trish and Faye are having fun with the animals, see if you can figure out what these clichés really mean. (See answers on page 24.)

They **TALK TURKEY** —with a turkey.

"Talking turkey" has been in use since at least 1840. The phrase may have come from a story about two hunters who were trying to decide who got to keep the turkey.

15

"How about those tickets?" Trish asks.

DO 'NOT FEED GOATS

"They're right at my fingertips", Faye says. "See?"

16

Oh, no! Trish and Faye
are CRUSHED.

Clichés often use active, physical words to describe inner feelings. Trish and Faye aren't really crushed—they haven't been injured. And the ground they're standing on hasn't moved an inch. But they *are* terribly disappointed.

The bottom has dropped out of their world.

Then **ALL OF A SUDDEN—**

Don't hit the panic button.

To hit or not hit the "panic button" is a saying that developed during *World War II*. It refers to airplane crews jumping out of their planes when there was only minor damage.

We've got you covered.

Clichés are catchy. They're easy to remember and say. (That's probably why they became clichés!) Here, three strangers are telling the girls not to worry, Help has arrived. Smile, girls!

Turn those frowns upside down!

Faye's **jaw drops.**

You could have **Knocked Trish over with a feather.**

Have you ever been so surprised that you let your mouth hang open? Or so shocked that you felt like you weren't in your body anymore? That's how Trish and Faye are feeling here.

The Bonus Brothers *themselves* give the girls new tickets!
And autographs too!

The concert is **A BLAST**–a dream come true.

"The Bonus Brothers **ROCK!**" Trish exclaims. "They **RULE!**"

"**Totally!**" Faye agrees.

Fifty years ago, people would have thought it strange to use the words *rock, rule,* and *totally.* But not anymore! Clichés are always changing, just like the rest of our language. BFN! (Bye for now!)

Cliché Charades

Gather a bunch of your friends together. Then have one person write down the following clichés, with their meanings, on strips of paper. This person will also be the scorekeeper and judge.

Take turns drawing a slip from a bowl. Act out the cliché, without speaking. The first person to guess what it is gets a point. If this person can also say what the cliché means, he or she gets two points.

He's like a bull in a china shop. (Someone who is clumsy and unaware of his surroundings.)

She's as busy as a bee. (Very busy; quickly moving from task to task.)

Does the cat have your tongue? (Don't be so quiet—say something!)

Don't count your chickens before they're hatched. (Don't plan on things that might not happen.)

That drives me up a wall! (Something that's really annoying.)

Look before you leap. (Think carefully about something before you do it.)

He slept like a log. (He slept very soundly.)

Stop and smell the roses. (Take time to enjoy the little things in life.)

To Learn More

More Books to Read

Cleary, Brian. *Skin Like Milk, Hair of Silk: What Are Similes and Metaphors?* Words Are CATegorical. Minneapolis: Millbrook Press, 2009.

Fandel, Jennifer. *Metaphors, Similes, and Other Word Pictures.* Understanding Poetry. Mankato, Minn.: Creative Education, 2005.

Leedy, Loreen. *Crazy Like a Fox: A Simile Story.* New York: Holiday House, 2008.

Internet Sites

FactHound offers a safe, fun way to find Internet sites related to this book. All of the sites on FactHound have been researched by our staff.

Here's all you do:
Visit *www.facthound.com*
Type in this code: 9781404862722

ANSWERS: "let the cat out of the bag": to tell a secret without meaning to; "let sleeping dogs lie": to leave something alone that may cause trouble if *not* left alone; "a wild goose chase": a pointless journey; "talk turkey": to talk about something in a direct, honest way

Glossary

exaggerate—to overstate something; for example, to describe something as being bigger or smaller than it actually is

expression—a group of words that are commonly used to tell an idea

idiom—a common saying that is special to a language or culture

phrase—a group of words that are used together

proverb—a short saying that tells an idea many people believe to be true

Index

Look for all the books in the Ways to Say It series:

She Sells Seashells and Other Tricky Tongue Twisters
Stubborn as a Mule and Other Silly Similes
Talking Turkey and Other Clichés We Say
You're Toast and Other Metaphors We Adore

Super-cool stuff! Check out projects, games and lots more at www.capstonekids.com